Los Angeles is Hideous

Los Angeles is Hideous

Poems About an Ugly City

By Andrew Heaton

Contents

The Greater L.A. Necroplex 1

Beaches are Overrated 3

If Pants Could Smirk 5

An Ode to Traffic 7

Fire Season 8

Congratulations for Putting Letters on a Hill 9

It's an Ugly Fucking Desert 11

Only Cowards Fear Winter 13

Homo Sapiens Siliconis 14

Villain du Jour 15

More About Cowards and Winter 17

Canyons Are Forbidden Trenches 19

Welcome to the Party 20

The Patron Saint of Asshats 21

Sprawl by Edict 23

Revival or Not, It's Still Ugly 25

There's Always a Goddamned Weedwhacker 26

Cthulhu's Fuckwit Brother 27

Springtime for Garbage 29

The Los Angeles "River" 30

Fame 31

The Big One 33

The Greater L.A. Necroplex

Pretty as a cinderblock smeared with lipstick
O blight of traffic and concrete dumpsters
Thy principle building material
Is bathroom tiling grout

Drenched in sunlight
As compensation
Like a chef at Applebee's
Drowning freeze-dried sadness in cheese
To hide the shame
The shame

All the beauty of a parking lot
And yet
Ironically
You will never find a parking space

Watch them toss palm trees at strip malls
To gussy up the streets
Like injecting Botox
Into a corpse

Behold the concrete slabs with squares gouged out
Where dreamers peek from cramped rooms
To gaze at hobos
Masturbating into open sewers

Hard square lines and jarring angles
Every neighborhood is the Used Tire District
Enjoy yon liquor store
With bars across the panes
There are no parks
But there are a lot of tent villages

Tis not a city
But a meatgrinder
That devours skinny hopefuls
And burps out chunks of porn star

Warm but humid
The wet spot on the bed
You just made with your crazy ex
Who's probably lying about birth control

Los Angeles is
A prison yard with sparklers
Chugging champagne beneath an overpass
A public toilet with a boob job
Instagram filters on a dead harlot

Beaches are Overrated

Yes, there's a beach
You twat
There are beaches everywhere

Drive an hour north
Or south
And there are still beaches
Only with less traffic
And cheaper rent

You could be a shoe salesman there, too
Or some other survival job
But keep more hard-earned cash
You won't, though
Because you're a moron
And think status can be gained through osmosis
By living in the same zip code
As famous people

It's one long goddamned beach
From here to fucking Alaska

But here, specifically!
Monthly rent is two thousand
And average salary is "exposure" and pocket change
Which leaves little in the way of food
Or a 401k
Because math

But there's a beach!
And I love beaches!
Because I enjoy
Getting sleepy
And hot
In a stretchy litter box
Near sharks and dead fish

My friend
Beaches are just deserts
With a hole at the end

If Pants Could Smirk

There are few men in Los Angeles
But a lot of 45-year-old boys
Who still wear hoodies
As if, perhaps
They recently graduated high school

Wear a collared shirt, a tie
And be mistaken as a waiter
The style here is skateboarding wunderkind

The kind of dumbass place
Where people buy designer bean bags
Or gold-plated sporks
And forget to set their watches

Flaunt the casual
As if to say
I am so successful
I can get away with t-shirts
Too aloof for slacks, am I
But please assume
I am too cool
To be aware of my own high status

Lapels?
Lapels are for adults

I am not an adult!
Adult means aging
I am young
I AM young!
I AM YOUNG!
So I wear a hoodie
Because I am so fresh and young!

Skinny jeans are fashion's answer
To "if pants could smirk"
And manboys don that denim fleshpaint
As to appear the more pubescent

My trousers say
"Job well executed"
and "I own a screwdriver"

An Ode to Traffic

If highways are a city's arteries
Los Angeles is begging for a heart attack
And a stroke so prodigious
It makes a popping noise
Audible in Arizona

A burgh most constipated
Squatting on a toilet
Straining, straining
To squeeze out a Prius

And when it succeeds
Teeth clenched, sweat drenched
Guess what?
The toilet is clogged
Because that's LA:
The septic tank of hope and dreams

Angelenos spend
128 hours in their cars
Each year
But it only takes an hour
To drive the fuck away

Fire Season

The horizon is burning oatmeal
Gasping ochre welkin
Inflamed bowels of dying sky gods

The sun is an orange smudge
Shouting against the anguished screams
Of dying trees

Because California is on fire
Again
In fact seasonally
The way other states have Autumn
Or when the peach blossums bloom
Except here, they explode

A thin layer of soot settles
On your 2004 Ford Taurus
Like the ashes of immolated angels
Or the smoking residue of dreams

Congratulations for Putting Letters on a Hill

Note her landmark:
A bunch of letters on a mound
As if some dyslexic deity
Tried to claim it for himself
Lest other trash gods stake it first

Spelt out atop Mount Lee
Named for a dead car dealer
It first read "Hollywoodland"
To advertise segregated housing
But now, simpler
HOLLYWOOD
To advertise hope, and cum

For awhile, it said
OLLYWOODLAND
When its caretaker got shitfaced
And drove off a cliff with the H

Then a stretch of time as
HuLLYW OD
As it splintered and rot
The road sign of Dorian Gray

Credit Hugh Hefner for its restoration
Rich through Playboy Magazine
Meaning the famous ivory letters are
Ultimately
Borne on the nips of countless, forgotten tits
Like the slaves who built the Pyramids

It's an Ugly Fucking Desert

If you look at the map on Google
And peer down on the city like an astronaut
Los Angeles has green!
Parks
Golf Courses
"Forests"

But on foot
(Or, rather, in a car)
It is all sun-blanched coffee grounds

Scrubby, desperate weeds
Dirt, dust, and candy wrappers
Blighted nothing, clogged with traffic

Hills, broken slags of scrubby brown
As if a mountain did chemotherapy
And then gave up, halfway through

Plenty of lush, green lawns, though
Which may be why
There's a water shortage
Because these morons
Moved to a fucking desert
Yet insist on pretending
It's basically Vermont

Los Angeles once had dense smog
Which has, thankfully, receded
Only to reveal
Why yes
It's still just heaps of squalor
Clumped atop cement
Used condoms on picnic tables

Cataract surgery is for naught
When peering into garbage

Only Cowards Fear Winter

The Arabs tell us:
Endless sunshine makes a desert
But more
Endless sunshine means no seasons
No Fall
Or Winter
So the years pass unnoticed
And time sneaks up on you
Until you wake up at forty
With roommates
And a hoodie
And go to your job
At the movie theater
Selling popcorn

Homo Sapiens Siliconis

Aging is shameful in La La Land
Old men smudge shoe polish in their hair
Old women pay alchemists
To stretch their faces
Like tent poles
Until weird, taut cheekbones
Make them look like cats

People here don't wrinkle
They just turn into plastic
And brown up like old saddlebags

There's nothing sadder than an old man
Wearing a starchy pelt atop his noggin
To camouflage honest pate
From fifty yards away

And nothing scarier
Than an aging lady
Who would rather be a hood ornament
Than risk laugh lines

Villain du Jour

O yonic horror,
We condemn thee
Rapist goblin!
Sexist fiend!
Harvey Weinstein, Bill Cosby, et cetera

Because

After twenty years of looking the other way
It's become convenient
To release our death grip on your coattails
And sling you under the bus

Count on us
To fight the good fight
And slay all the monsters
When monster-slaying is trendy
And bears no cost
Or risk
And we're pretty sure everyone else is, too

Otherwise... nah

But to be clear
We still think Kansas is sexist
And we are better than you

[Applause]

More About Cowards and Winter

If ancient frost giants
Could be swayed to wander
To this lump of sunshine and tarmac
And shivered the floodlit wastelands

Half the folk would ward off winter
By forsaking gluten
As Flagellants did sin
To forestall the Bubonic Plague

While the smarter half
Would spring to action
(And with great volume)
((And sanctimony))
(((And hashtags)))
To compel Sacramento
To change the freezing point
By law

Fortunately, there is Los Angeles
Where those who are too febrile
To countenance sleet
May carry their purse dogs
And mildewed fantasies
Through a balmy 70 degrees

Welcome to the Party

Hello!
Fun party
I'm Brian
What do you do?

Oh.

I have to go

Canyons Are Forbidden Trenches

I will admit
There are stately abodes
In Beachwood Gutter
And Laurel Socket
But we will never dwell there

What is a canyon, but a maw?
Separating the repugnant
From the vapid

Putter through yon asphalt trench
And emerge, blinking, amongst the suburbs
Swollen with McMansions
As if spaceships from Planet Asshole
Crashlanded
Onto Planet Ugly

You will never live nor sup
In the glossy boxes perched amongst
The city's stylish canyons

Although with a little luck
And a little surgery
Your hot friend might

If you luck out
You can snag a house
In distant burbs
Like a hermit crab
Skittering with relief
Into a slightly nicer beer can

The Patron Saint of Asshats

Dear Moron,

With the t-shirt
of Che Guevara
    So youthful
    So rebellious
    So iconic

Know ye of the gays he sent to labor camps?
Or his dearest want
To obtain the atom bomb
With which to whelm New York?
It would have pissed off Wall Street, I guess
But also killed a lot of toddlers

No matter
It's not a manifesto
Just a t-shirt
With something trendy upon it printed
So you can get credit for being edgy
With all the people who agree with you
And then go back to doing nothing

It says:
"I am a rebel!"
Against corporations
Like the one I bought this t-shirt from

It says:
I care more about romantic haircuts
And proto-memes
Than understanding problems
Or volunteering
Or researching the subject
Of this shallow apparel

I don't want to hear another goddamned word
About how I'm "greedy"
For preferring charity
        Which I give
Over taxes
        Which I pay
From trust fund kids who do neither
Yet always have money
For improv class

Sprawl by Edict

Los Angeles, cursed
Oozes across the map
Like maple syrup on a sidewalk
Or cellulite
In the beer belly
Of a cyclops

Not a single polis
But several
Tumored into each other
With no center
Or reprieve

How so?
Back in the 40s
The city fathers cobbled laws
Banning multi-family dwellings

To keep out the Blacks

The logic was:
Black people like apartment buildings (?)
So let's just not have any

Instead, let us forge
Neighborhood Covenants
Where homeowners may veto "undesirables"
From moving in

Today, there are black people
And yet!
The law persists:
You cannot build up
You can only build out

A swarm of strip malls
Connected by asphalt
Traffic congestion
And zip codes

O Los Angeles
Though art governed
By the ghosts of bigots past
Who caged the sky
With zoning ordinances

Their echo summons sprawl

Revival or Not, It's Still Ugly

Mission Revival
And Spanish Colonial Revival
Are filthy lies
Whispered by real estate agents
To etch dimples
onto dilapitaded shoe boxes
And lubricate them
with pastel paint

To confuse you into thinking
Maybe
Somehow
You're in Granada!
Or Quintana Roo

But you are only in Los Angeles
And just spent $36
On waffles

There's Always a Goddamned Weedwhacker

They say you can hear the ocean in a seashell

Should you nestle your ear against a hubcap
You will hear the song of Los Angeles
The eternal hiss of carburetors
Sucking down dinosaur juice and farting toxins
Honking at each other
Like asshole robot geese

Put down the hubcap
There are plenty
Also mufflers
And syringes

Hear that?

It's a weedwhacker
There's always a weedwhacker
There's always a goddamned weedwhacker

Cthulhu's Fuckwit Brother

The Titans wail, imprisoned
In the sorrowed depths of Tartarus
As far below Hades
As Hades is from us

I would rather loose them all
Upon our unsuspecting world
With their monstrous snapping heads
And cosmic bloodlust
Than stir awake
Whatever jackfuck deity
Kips beneath Los Angeles
Like a pothead slunk under a beanbag

Observe that city numen
That slacked-jawed concrete gargoyle
Sleeping off his coke binge
Snoring through five million engines
His dandruff flowing hither and yon
Through discarded wrappers, rubbish, and rubbers

Every strip mall is a hickey
Upon his calloused asphalt skin
From a gummy, stinking Gorgon
Who slunk out of Hell's worst dive bar
To lick his twitching varicose veins
Of never-ending traffic

Savages on certain islands
Toss supple virgins into volcanoes
To sate the petty gods therein
But in our enlightened culture
We lob hotties at Los Angeles
To keep her nethergod drowsy

Springtime for Garbage

Litter is the pollen of garbage
And it's always allergy season here
Wrappers, plastic, soggy paper
Scuffling across the blight
Like fuckwit tumbleweeds
Or the chaff of fast food
Which clump, exhausted
Beneath overpasses
As if a pregnant landfill miscarried

I like to call litter
"Goblin confetti"
And imagine green little bastards
Performing merry gutter jigs
Amongst the fluttering offal
Like Tibetan prayer flags
Supplicating the God of Spilth

The Los Angeles "River"

Behold!
The mighty Los Angeles River
A lengthy concrete drainage ditch
Wide as a shoebox
Pretty as a penal shower
Dribbling pollution into the sea

If a river but trickles
Through a mortared gutter
Is it a river at all?
Or just a leak
From some distant, dehydrated mountain
With an engorged prostate
And bad aim

Twice a year
The rain gets lost
Or drunk
And shambles through LA
Sloshing life back into this trough

But the rest of the time
It's merely the seepage
Of urban incontinence

Fame

Horace tells me
"They change their sky
But not their soul
Who run across the sea"

I tell you
Those who lust for fame
And secure it
Are still the awkward sweaty kid
At the middle school dance

Thinketh:
       Fame will solve for sex
       Fame will solve for cash
       Fame will solve for me

For surely, we can fix a wobbly stool
By draping it in velvet
And plug our leaky bucket
If only we had more water
With which to sate its hole

I have met actors
Who live in hovels
(With roommates!)
And make money as medical test subjects
And in porn
Or worse, as background extras
To buy lottery tickets for a jackpot of stardom

My friends
We could have stayed
Back home
In Nowheresville
Near our parents
Gone into community theater together, at night
Respected by our peers
Creatively fulfilled
Yet also
Had mortgages

The Big One

One day
The tectonic plates themselves
Will shudder

At the ugliness
The traffic
The cost
The cilantro

And the city will wail and clatter
Like Jenga blocks at closing time

Sayeth "Earthquake"?
Nay.
The Earth itself is gagging

When she finally retches hard enough
And lets loose The Big One
This wretched people clot
This horrid asphalt carbuncle
Will slough into the drink
And the prophets shall proclaim:

Lo, the Earth hath given herself
An enema

DEDICATION

For Lumbercon:

Nick, Chloe, Other Nick, Kim, Kevin,
Jenny, Krepow, and Jared

Thank you for the laughs, the friendship, and that
lovely decorative axe you all gave me. Still have that axe.

AFTERWARD

Please accept my apologies; I am not a poet. I am a comedian writing a parody of poetry.

I confess I don't even particularly understand the concept. It seems to me you should either write a good, respectable adult paragraph—with indentions and semicolons and possibly diagrams—or just bang out a song. Frankly I don't understand how poetry still even *exists*, since songs are basically just poems you can whistle. From what I can tell "poems" are song lyrics written by people too lazy to learn guitar. I guess they made sense before instruments were invented, but banjos have been around, what, four hundred years? No wonder Neil Diamond has sex on tap but nobody knows who the current Poet Laureate is, possibly even including the Poet Laureate.

Where was I? Right. In the event that I am wrong, and poems are not merely unformed song fetuses whispered by people in coffee shops who unironically own berets, then: I apologize. As a comedian I am frequently enraged by civilians who assume they "could have been a comedian, but just didn't feel like it," and assume there's no real skill or craft involved. No doubt poetry has all sorts of depth and artistry I am utterly blind to, and a real, legitimate poet would burst into flame if they so much as touched this coffee table book in the process of trying to flatten a wasp.

Finally, with regards to Los Angeles, I'm sure there are some redeeming features I would have discovered if I'd stuck around the city long enough without eventually hanging myself. One of my friends assures me that "Los Angeles is fantastic, it just takes eight years or so to appreciate." The great comedian Patton Oswalt writes: "Los Angeles is five of the best cities in the country, and three or four of the worst."

It's been a pleasure to write about those "three or four of the worst," and oddly satisfying to discover that sometimes the Muses visit us resplendent and breathy and shrouded in light, and sometimes they creep up around closing time, all warty and gassy—yet are inspiring nonetheless.

Cheers!

Andrew Heaton

April, 2021
2,449 miles from Los Angeles

P.S. I would specifically like to apologize to Nick and Krepow, who live in Los Angeles. And to Chloe, who has kin there. Oh, and Andrew Young, who didn't quite make the cut for dedication in this book, but simultaneously insists on living in Los Angeles and being friends with me at the same time. Apologies for slagging your hood, sir!

ABOUT THE AUTHOR

Andrew Heaton lived in Los Angeles twice, but escaped both times.

He lived in a tool shed behind his best friend's house while working as a background extra between 2008 – 2009.

He then returned (to network!) and signed an expensive year-long lease exactly two weeks before the Covid lockdown. Heaton realized that, absent career opportunity or financial incentive, Los Angeles is actually big stinking, expensive desert filled with beautiful people and ugly buildings. After several torturous months he faked his own death and escaped to the United States, where he now resides.

Heaton is the host of *The Political Orphanage*, which is a thinky policy podcast thing.

He is the author of the best-selling political satire *Laughter Is Better Than Communism,* as well as two funny novels: *Frank Got Abducted* (about aliens) and *Happier as Werewolves* (about werewolves).

To stalk him, visit www.mightyheaton.com

Made in the USA
Las Vegas, NV
18 July 2021

26627897R00028